a $mart girl's guide to
money

W9-BNA-607

how to make it, save it, and spend it

by Nancy Holyoke
illustrated by Ali Douglass

★ American Girl®

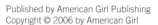

Published by American Girl Publishing

Questions or comments? Call 1-800-845-0005,
visit our Web site at **americangirl.com**, or write to Customer Service,
American Girl, 8400 Fairway Place, Middleton, WI 53562.

Printed in China
12 13 14 15 16 17 LEO 20 19 18 17 16

Editorial Development: Sara Hunt
Art Direction and Design: Chris Lorette David
Production: Kendra Schluter, Mindy Rappe, Jeannette Bailey, Judith Lary
Consultants: Carol Malanowski, Chris Spencer, Glen Allen, and
Janet Garkey, Center for Personal Finance, Credit Union National
Association, Inc.
Illustrations: Ali Douglass

This book is not intended to replace the advice of financial planners and tax
advisors. It should be considered an additional resource only.

Library of Congress Cataloging-in-Publication Data
Holyoke, Nancy.
A $mart girl's guide to money: how to make it, save it, and spend it / by
Nancy Holyoke ; illustrated by Ali Douglass.
p. cm.
ISBN 978-1-59369-103-5
1. Girls—Finance, Personal—Juvenile literature. I. Title: Smart girl's guide to
money. II. Title: Girl's guide to money. III. Douglass, Ali, ill.
IV. Title.
HG179.H5946 2006
332.0240083'42—dc 22   2005058909

Dear Reader:

When you were little, you didn't have to think about money. Your parents took care of that. But now you have some money of your own, and you're making more of your own decisions about what to do with it. If you're like most girls, some of those decisions have been smart and some haven't. You know that being "money smart" feels better.

In fact, being money smart can feel great. How come?

Money's a tool. People use it to get the things that they want the most in life—freedom, opportunity, comfort, good health, safety, and pleasure. They also use it to avoid the things they want least—things like poverty, fear, stress, and hunger. Having money won't necessarily make you happy, but knowing how to use it wisely can help you build a future that will.

This book is packed with tips on how to make, save, and spend money. It includes lots of quizzes, advice from girls like you, and a list of over a hundred different money-making ideas. You'll even find business cards and other printable items to use on the job at a special *Smart Girl's Guide to Money* link at americangirl.com.

Put it all together and you'll be amazed at how much easier it is to get what you want from your money. You have big dreams about what you can do and accomplish in this world, and we hope this book does a thing or two to help you achieve them.

Your friends at American Girl

contents

a girl and her money

Money. It's great to have, fun to spend, and (for some of us, anyway) hard to keep.

Think how much money's flowed through your hands already in your lifetime. Take just this month. There's your allowance, the $10 a week you get for lunch, the money your parents gave you for the movies, and the check your Aunt Maud sent for your birthday. That's $100 in four short weeks! Why, there could be $1,000 a year coming and going through your very own wallet. Who knew?

Yet if you stop and think about it, there is money flowing in and out of pockets all around you. Where does it all come from?

In a word: work. If you have a quarter in your pocket, it's because at some point someone earned it—maybe you, maybe your parents, maybe someone else. But someone.

money moments

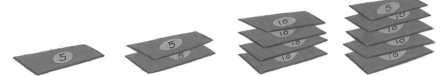

Money influences how we see other people and how we see ourselves. Maybe that's why the decisions we make about it often have more to do with emotion than with math.

7:55

"Here's your allowance," says Sierra's mother. "Don't spend it all on something silly." Sierra nods. She'll try, but if Morgan and Amber want to go to the mall after school, she can't exactly say no.

9:30

Amber is smiling as she walks down the hall. Yesterday, she figured out she'd earned $253 selling ankle bracelets since September. $253 of her very own! She feels like she grew two inches overnight. She decides she'll spend $5 after school. She can afford it.

11:16

Genevieve has a new purse. Sierra knows for a fact that her brother's car cost less than that brand of purse. She decides Genevieve is stuck-up.

1:36

"Cool shoes," says Amber to Morgan. "How much did they cost?" The real answer is a lot, but Morgan knows her family has more money than Amber's. "I'm not sure," she says. "I think they were on sale."

The girls have been at the mall for an hour. Morgan and Amber both bought something. "You've got to get something, too, Sierra," they say. Sierra does.

The credit-card bill has arrived. Amber's parents argue for a while. Then doors slam. Amber puts music on her boom box, sits on her bed, and makes ankle bracelets.

No clean laundry for Morgan tonight. The washer's broken. "Let's get a new one," says her dad. "It's only money."

Sierra is reading in bed. It's a story about an orphan who gets adopted by a millionaire. She falls asleep imagining what it would be like to be that rich. Next week she'll save her allowance for sure. Maybe.

money emotions

You've probably had all kinds of feelings about money.

confidence

happiness

jealousy

pride

guilt

greed

anxiety

You also have habits and attitudes that have been shaped by your family. A girl whose parents talk with ease about family finances will think differently about money than a girl whose parents worry or argue when the bills arrive. A girl who's grown up shopping the sales with her mom will likely have different spending habits than a girl who has only seen her mom buy freely. A girl's experiences may incline her to like or dislike people with more money—or to like or dislike people with less.

All this means that your feelings about money may be complicated. But the way you *use* money doesn't have to be.

When it comes to making decisions about money, keep your head cool and your thinking clear. Let three basic questions be your guide:

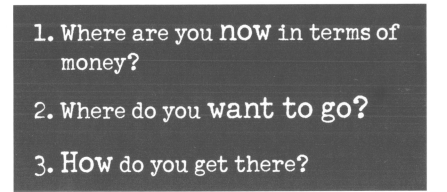

1. Where are you now in terms of money?

2. Where do you want to go?

3. How do you get there?

allowance

A lot of girls get their first experience managing money when they first get an allowance. Here's what some girls have to say about how it works in their homes:

"I only get an allowance when I do all my chores, like feeding the animals, putting my laundry away, and just picking up after myself. Chores are not my favorite pastime, but I do love my allowance!"
Abigail

"Kids should do chores around the house but not for an allowance. Our parents cook, clean, and drive us to school. The least we can do is help out a little without asking for money."
Kelly

"I do not get an allowance. I don't ask for one because my parents buy me everything. If I want to go to the movies, my parents give me the money."
Alexis

"Allowance should be a privilege, not a right. Kids should do something for their allowance."
Jesek

"I get an allowance of $10 a week. I have to pay for my own clothes. That has taught me a lot about responsibility."
Joley

"I get an allowance. My mom likes the fact that I am not bugging her for money. Having my own money has helped me learn how to manage money."
Alex

"My dad gives my brother and me $12 for allowance. Then he makes us pay $4 for 'taxes.' Another $4 goes toward savings. The last $4 we get to keep. So you could say that when all of our 'bills' are paid, we get $4."
Jessica

"I earn my allowance. It's a great reward for doing your chores and getting good grades. Allowance is also good because it teaches you the value of money."
Nicole

How to get a raise

Do you think you should get more allowance? How you talk to your parents will be key.

• Pick a good time to talk. If your dad is talking on the phone and trying to feed peas to the baby, that is not the moment to march in and make your case.

• Don't rely on comparisons. If you get 50¢ and every girl you know gets $5, O.K.—you can point that out. But if you get $5 and you've got a friend who gets $8, save your breath. Most parents want to use their own judgment—not the neighbors'.

• Say you'll do extra work around the house. If it's your job to sweep the kitchen after dinner, offer to load the dishwasher, too. If you give more, you may get more.

• Say you'll pay for more of your expenses. Your parents might think it's a good deal if you start paying for your own movies and treats.

• Show your parents that you're responsible with the money you already have. Most adults are going to feel better about giving money to a girl who saves a third of her allowance than they are to a girl who blows her entire wad at the mall every payday.

• Accept no for an answer. Your family's financial situation could make it impossible for your parents to give you more in allowance. Your parents also might just disagree with you about what the right amount should be. Either way, if you keep your cool and accept their decision with good grace, it could help you a year from now when you ask again. For now, turn your mind to ways to make money on your own.

your $ style

Which sounds more like you? Circle your answers.

1. "Where's that gift card you got for your birthday?" asks your mom. You say:

    a. "In my dresser drawer. I'm still thinking about what I want."

    b. "Beats me." (In fact, it's under your bed along with a petrified Twizzler and some dust balls the size of Chicago.)

2. "That will be four dollars," says the sales-woman. You:

    a. hand her the money.

    b. say, "Uh—" You didn't check the prices. You have only $2.51.

3. You keep your money:

    a. in the bank on your desk.

    b. in piles all over your room. And at the bottom of your backpack. And in the pockets of the clothes you wore yesterday. There may be some on the floor of the car, too.

4. "How much did you spend at the game?" asks your dad. You:

    a. tell him.

    b. check your pockets. Everything, evidently.

5. You've done it again—left your gloves someplace. You:

   a. **check the lost-and-found and everyplace else you can think of.**

   b. **borrow your brother's. You can always get new gloves.**

6. "Here's your change," says the clerk. You:

   a. **put the bills neatly into your wallet.**

   b. **toss bills and coins into the open mouth of your purse. Bombs away!**

Answers

If you answered mostly **b's,** you're operating as if money and the things it buys have no value. But they do. Would you walk into a store and knowingly pay $5 for a $3 pen? Not likely. Yet if you go through the world blind to the value of what you've got, the results may be about the same. You're losing out.

If you answered mostly **a's,** you're not just tidy, you're knowledgeable. You know how much money you have. You know what you're spending. You know what's left. Keeping track gives you a better sense of what the money in your purse is really worth. When you see a snazzy barrette at the checkout, you'll not only know whether you have enough money to buy it but whether you really should.

a big truth

Money smarts begin with

good habits

and

just plain paying attention.

making money

HANDMADE Magnets & Bracelets!

going into business

You've been thinking: your allowance is small, and your ideas about what you'd like to do with your money are big. So maybe it's time you went to work and made some money of your own. But what can you do? Where do the good moneymaking ideas come from?

Yours will come from **you.**

Start by **looking around.** A good moneymaker gives people something they want or need. Are there 18 dogs on your block?

There could be an opportunity for a dog walker. Are there 18 little kids?

Then you might consider babysitting or adapting your juggling act for children's parties.

Better yet: **talk to the neighbors.** Ask them to name three things that need doing around their homes that they don't have the time or desire to do—three tasks they would pay someone else to complete. Make a list. **Sit down with your mom or dad** and talk about whether there is anything on the list that you could do.

Remember that there are two basic ways to make money: **selling services** and **selling products.** If you can't think of a service, maybe you can produce a product.

Whatever you come up with, be sure to **check out the competition**. If there are three girls selling hot drinks outside the soccer tournament already, you might want to try selling something else. If that boy who's always raked the courthouse lawn is moving to Tallahassee, now could be the perfect time to take his place.

How's your **timing?** If you want to make money in December, wrapping gifts would be ideal. If you want to make money in the summer, you'd be better off weeding gardens.

Finally, ask yourself what you *want* to do. What ideas excite you the most? Your **enthusiasm** will make it easier to work hard, produce a better product, and do a better job.

is it the right job for you?

What sounds most like you? Circle your answers.

1. "Dear Mom and Dad," you write your first week at camp. "My favorite thing so far is . . ."

   a. hanging around the cabin talking to friends.

   b. doing mosaics at the craft hut.

   c. swimming and horseback riding.

   d. learning about animal tracks.

   e. singing around the campfire.

2. It's Saturday. None of your friends are around. You:

   a. blow bubbles with the three-year-old next door.

   b. make bread.

   c. go out and shoot some hoops in the driveway.

   d. mess around on your computer.

   e. write a story.

3. There are five of you working on a project for the medieval fair. You volunteer to:

   a. sit at the booth and talk to people.

   b. make a castle out of foam core.

   c. do the shopping and all the setup.

   d. research castle life.

   e. design the banner and play the recorder.

4. It's your mom's birthday. You want to give her something special. You:

   a. ask her best friends over for a night playing board games.

   b. make her breakfast in bed.

   c. plan a long bike ride and picnic.

   d. find out what happened in the news the day she was born and create a newspaper on your computer.

   e. paint her a picture.

5. In your wildest dreams, you see yourself 20 years from now as:

   a. the President of the United States, working with other people to make the world a better place.

   b. a doctor, doing open-heart surgery.

   c. a mountaineering guide on Mount Everest.

   d. the youngest chemist ever to win the Nobel Prize.

   e. a movie star who writes and illustrates children's books and plays the bassoon in her spare time.

Answers

People person

If you answered mostly **a's,** you love being around people. You might be a good salesperson. You might like to take lunches to old Mr. Wigwag or ride herd on the quintuplets next door. You get energy from other people, and they get energy from you.

Hands-on and handy

If you answered mostly **b's,** you like doing things with your hands. That might mean baking cupcakes for the fair, making decoupage photo frames, or braiding necklaces. Find something people want that you can make well in a reasonable amount of time for a reasonable amount of money. Then get to work.

Mover and shaker

If you answered mostly **c's,** physical activity is important to you. Jobs that get you out of the house and keep you moving might be good—anything from teaching sports to delivering flyers for Ms. Loofa at the yoga studio or organizing the Messerschmitts' garage. Keep it active.

Think tank

If you answered mostly **d's,** you get a kick out of using your head. You like solving puzzles and knowing how things work. You might like designing Web pages for school clubs. You might like setting up an aquarium for your aunt the dentist, or tutoring little Billy Beasley from down the street. Look for a job where you can use your brains, patience, and know-how to help others figure things out.

Expressive

If you answered mostly **e's,** expressing yourself is important to you. Moneymakers that involve music, dance, art, or theater might be just the thing. Whether you're performing in front of a crowd, putting the finishing touches on a movie, or designing a garden, you will enjoy sharing your vision of the world and creating something new.

For more help finding the perfect job, see the list of "101 Moneymaking Ideas" starting on page 87.

will it work?

Your idea is a perfect fit. So far, so good. Now you have to figure out if your moneymaking idea is practical: you have to be sure it works. So pull up a chair, grab some paper, and sharpen a pencil.

Start by writing down everything you need for this project and think—*really* think—about how you're going to get it.

Skills and training
You want to be good at what you're selling. Do you have all the skills you need to do the job? If not, how can you learn them?

Partners
Are you doing this alone or do you need help? If you want a partner, pick someone dependable who's as interested in the job as you are. Your friend Megan may be lots of fun, but if she was putting straws up her nose at lunch while you were describing your moneymaker, you'd be better off asking someone else.

Tools and supplies
List everything you need to make your product or perform your service. Do you have these things? Where will you get them?

Money
How much are those tools and supplies going to cost you? Where will you get that money? Do you need to borrow from someone? Who will that be? How long will it take you to make the money to pay the person back?

Permission
Having a car wash at the gas station may be a great idea, but you can't do it without the owner's permission. Do you have it?

Time
How much time do you have to devote to your moneymaker? Be honest. You've got homework and other activities. There'll be trouble down the road if you're always counting on your mom and dad to bail you out.

Safety
Is the activity safe? The only acceptable answer is "yes."

Other basics
Do you need transportation? Anything else? Write it down.

Advertising
How will you let your customers know you exist? You could use flyers, posters, business cards, T-shirts, or yard signs. You could also put notices in newsletters or other publications.

Remember that advertising works only if the right people see it. So if you're making, say, cat toys, put your advertising someplace cat owners are sure to go, like pet stores and veterinary offices (ask first).

Pricing
What are you going to charge for your product or service? What do your competitors charge? You can't charge less money than it took you to make your item, but you can't charge a lot more than the competition charges, either, unless your item or service is better than theirs.

Mikala's Pretzels

Skills and training
* Check out soft pretzel recipes on the Internet. Pick a few and try them.

Tools and supplies
* Basic ingredients $9
* Cinnamon?   ✓
* Parmesan cheese? $3

Total $12

Advertising
* Design flyers on the computer.

Everything still look good? All right. Now let's see if you'll make a profit. Your profit isn't the money you take in from your customers. It's the money you take in (your income) minus the money you spent to make that money (your expenses). Got that? It's really very easy.

First, think about how much you're going to be **bringing in.** What are you going to charge? How much of your product do you plan to sell each month? How many times will you perform your service?

Then consider what you will have to spend in an average month to keep your business going. For instance, you might have **ongoing expenses** like cooking ingredients, gas for the mower, or film for your camera.

Talk to your parents about **taxes.** If you make over a certain amount every year, you may also have to pay taxes.

You may also need to use some of your earnings to repay your parents for the **money you borrowed** to get started.

And of course you can't forget **your friend** who's been laboring away beside you.

So, say you're making elephant earrings. The whole thing might shake out something like this:

Income

What I will charge for my earrings __$10__

In one month, I expect to sell __20__ pairs of earrings

My TOTAL monthly income will be __$200__

Expenses

What I will have to spend in an average
month to do business:

elephant charms __$30__

beads and loops __$10__

What I will have to spend in an average month
to advertise and promote my business __$10__

Other monthly expenses __0__

My TOTAL monthly expenses will be __$50__

Profit

$$\underset{\text{my income}}{\$200} - \underset{\text{my expenses}}{\$50} = \underset{\text{my profit before taxes}}{\$150}$$

After I pay my taxes $150 – $23 = $127
and pay back my loans $127 – $17 = $110
and split the profits with my partner $110 ÷ 2 = $55

I will have (ta-da!) ($55) as my own profit.

parts & partners

As you can see, a business may involve all kinds of different tasks. If you're going solo, you'll have lots of different hats to wear. If you have partners, you can talk about how to divide up the work.

Business manager
Your job is to keep track of the money. You'll write down expenses and income and make sure you're making a profit.

Marketing
Your job is to sell your business to customers. You'll create a good image for the business, use advertising to make sure the right people know about it, and attract customers with promotions and special deals.

Design
Does this business sell pot holders? Then somebody's got to decide what the pot holders look like. That would be you.

Production

You produce what the business sells: you weave the pot holders, print the bumper stickers, or bake the snickerdoodles.

Customer service

Your job is to make the customer glad she came so that she'll come back again—and again. Questions and complaints (and compliments!) go to you.

Friends

No matter what roles you're playing, you and your partners are friends before anything else. Make sure it stays that way. Be fair with one another. If you plan to split the money equally, everyone should do equal amounts of work. Cooperate, especially in busy and stressful times. Don't be bossy. Have a weekly or monthly meeting where you talk over problems and solve them together.

starting up

Once you know what you're doing, do it with style.

Find a great name
Why settle for a plain name when with a little effort you can think of one that's catchy, meaningful, or amusing?

Create a great image
Design a logo to go with your name. A logo is a picture or symbol that represents your business. You can use a logo in all kinds of places—on advertisements, stationery, and business cards. Like the name, it should express the spirit of your business.

Promote yourself

Advertising isn't the only way you can promote your moneymaker. Offer special deals to first-time customers. Hand out free samples. People may need an extra reason to try out a new business. Give them one.

For business cards and other printable items you can use for your business, go to the *Smart Girl's Guide to Money* link at americangirl.com.

Set the terms

Be sure your customer knows what you're charging before you do the job.

For certain moneymakers, you might want to have a client sign a contract that spells out all the details of the agreement to avoid confusion. Write up a single contract that you can use with all your clients (get help from your mom or dad). Include a space to write in the date you make the agreement with the client, a space for the date the service is being delivered, and a space for your client's signature. Keep the contract stored on your computer and print out a new copy for every job. That makes it easy.

Get references

Do you have some happy clients? Ask a few if they'd be willing to write a short letter of recommendation that you could show to people who are thinking about hiring you for the first time. Perhaps these kind folks would allow you to give out their phone number as well. The words of a satisfied client can mean a lot.

Make it fun

Above all, have some fun with what you're doing. Be creative. Show some spirit. Make things fresh. It will give your moneymaker a distinctive personality that customers will remember. It will also make things far more entertaining for you.

Contract

Date: May 15

Client: Ms. Margaret Mullet, 1111 Whiting Lane

Party details: A birthday party for Willie Mullet from 3:30–5:00 on June 1 at the client's home

Guests: About six 5-year-olds

Services provided: Paige will arrive an hour before party time to put up decorations. The party will have a fish theme. Paige will oversee the party. Games will include "Pin the Fin on the Fish" and hitting a shark piñata. Guests will fish over a sheet for party favors before Paige leads everyone outside to run through the sprinkler. Paige will also serve the food and clean up afterward.

Services not provided: Client will provide decorations, shark piñata, paper goods, party favors, and food. Client will be at home during the party.

Fee: $25. Please pay at the end of the party.

I agree to these terms:

Margaret B. Mullet

are you innovative?

Which sounds like something you'd do? Circle your answers.

A. The dog's clean and brushed and all ready for the Fourth of July parade, just like your neighbors wanted. You:

   1. **take her home.**

   2. **tie a red, white, and blue bow around her neck and then take her home.**

   3. **tie a red, white, and blue bow around her neck and take her home with a bagful of dog treats.**

B. After you mow a lawn you:

   1. **leave.**

   2. **give the homeowner a business card (your logo is a sheep with grass in its mouth) and then leave.**

   3. **ask the owner if you can put a little sign in the yard that reads, "This lawn was mowed by Yolanda's Yards," then give him your card and leave.**

C. You knew you could make these picture frames when you saw the craft in a magazine. You:

   1. **make them exactly as they were shown in the magazine.**

   2. **figure out how to make different shapes and sizes.**

   3. **figure out how to make different shapes and sizes, add new materials, and then keep track of which frames sell best so that you can continue making changes.**

D. You'd love to babysit for the kids next door, but they already have a regular babysitter. You:

1. **give up and watch TV.**

2. **find out that the kids need help in math and ask the parents if they'd hire you as a homework helper.**

3. **find out that the kids need help in math, print up a flyer for your new homework-helper business, and hand-deliver the flyer both to the people next door and to other families you know and like.**

E. Uh-oh. You thought you'd been making money. In fact, you spent more on the ingredients for this ice cream than you made selling it. You:

1. **forget *that* business.**

2. **figure out how to make more money by switching from cones to banana splits.**

3. **figure out how to make more money by switching from cones to banana splits—and even more by adding a "Mount Fuji," where you bury the banana in whipped cream for an extra dollar, to the menu.**

Answers

Add up the numbers you circled. The **higher** your score, the more inventive you tend to be. Being inventive, or innovative, with a business is a good thing. No, actually, it's a great thing. Why? Because it will help you take an ordinary product and make it something special. It will help you take advantage of opportunities to promote yourself. It will help you change what you're doing to suit the situation. When problems arise, being inventive will help you solve them.

If your score is toward the **low end,** don't despair. A knack for problem solving isn't something a person is born with. In a lot of ways, it's a matter of training yourself to look twice at a situation— or three or four times. It's a matter of stopping to wonder if there's a better way to do it. So trust yourself more. Bounce some ideas off your friend Jasmine or your cousin Joyce. Get ideas from customers. Let yourself be a little playful. You'll be surprised how many ideas you'll find if you take the time to look.

home office

A few easy tricks will help you keep track of business once your moneymaker is up and running.

Get a special **appointment calendar.** Keep the calendar handy and write down your appointments as soon as they're made.

You'll want a **list of clients' names and phone numbers,** too. If you charge more for babysitting at a house with five kids than you charge for babysitting at a house with one, note those different rates on this sheet so that you don't forget.

An **invoice** is a bill. In some businesses, invoices can come in handy. Say five people have hired you to shovel snow off their driveways. Those people might not always be home when you arrive with your shovel. An invoice left in the door will remind them that they owe you money—and keeping a copy of the invoice in a file at home will remind you to ask again if they don't pay.

Keep **good records** of everything you do, especially of bills and receipts.

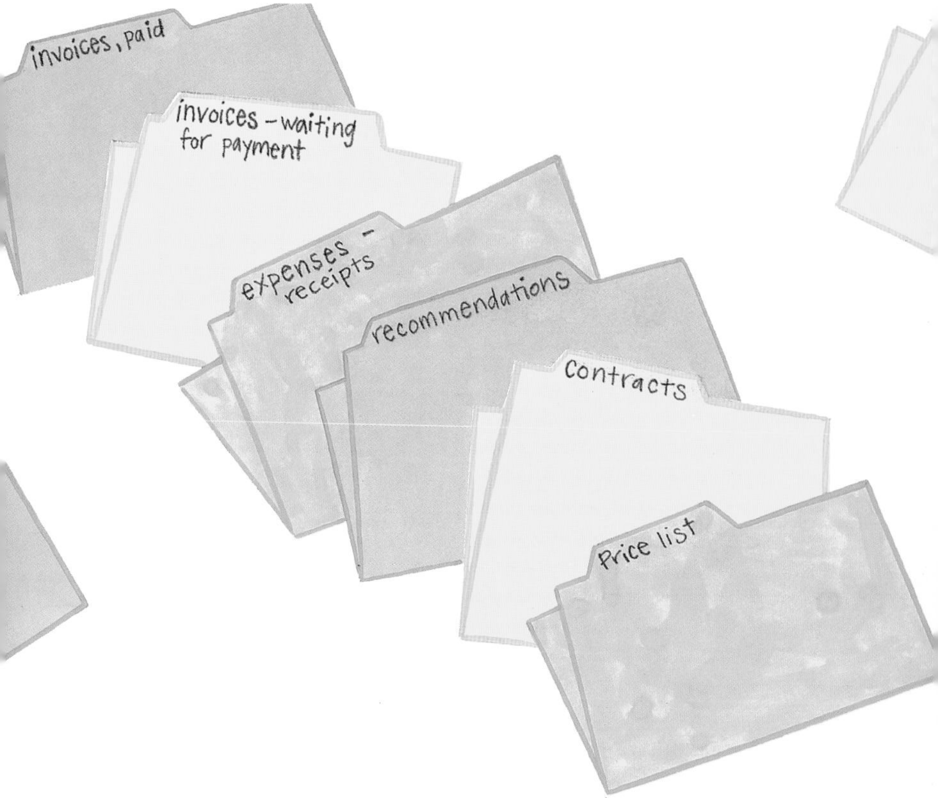

invoices, paid

invoices – waiting for payment

expenses – receipts

recommendations

contracts

Price list

Finally, keep track of your money in a **ledger**.

date	description	money out	money in	balance
			$30.00	$30.00
7/15	loan from Mom			$22.36
7/28	baking supplies	$7.64		
7/30	sold cookies		$15.50	$37.86
8/5	baking supplies	$12.92		$24.94
8/7	sold cookies		$22.75	$47.69
8/8	loan payment	$10.00		$37.69
8/10	advertising	$8.00		$29.69

keeping the customer happy ☺

You worked hard to get your customers. You want to keep them. Here's how:

Honor your appointments. **Be on time.** If you're running late, call and say so.

Be **polite, respectful, and upbeat.** Smile. Say "please" and "thank you." Dress appropriately and be clean and neat.

Get the instructions. If you're cleaning Mrs. Houdini's basement, **listen carefully** to what she tells you. Ask questions. Make notes if it will help you remember. Be sure you know exactly what she wants and doesn't want.

That said, don't expect your client to tell you everything. If the drought is killing Mr. Lobelia's flowers while you're bringing in the mail during his vacation, go ahead and water them. If you find rain coming in an open window at the Weatherwaxes' when you stop by to walk the dog, close it. **Anticipate trouble and show initiative.**

Be reliable. **Keep your promises.** If you've said you'd do something, do it. Follow through and be consistent.

Do a little extra without being asked. Stay a little longer or offer a little more. Everybody likes to get **more for less.**

Reward good customers with special deals. Let them know you appreciate their business.

Guarantee your work. If the earring you made fell apart, replace it. If you forgot to wash the mudroom floor, wash it the next time for free. Listen to complaints and admit your mistakes. Do what you can to make things right for the customer.

Be fair. Set reasonable prices.

Be honest.

Be better. If you're selling cupcakes, make sure they're good cupcakes. If you're washing windows, wash them well. If you're selling birdhouses, be sure they're well made. You want customers to come away knowing they can trust you.

troubleshooting

Got a problem? Don't let it shut you down. Just take a deep breath, then figure out how to fix it.

No go

You know what you want to do for your moneymaker: give cheerleading lessons. But your mom won't let you do it!

Politely ask for her reasons. If she's worried about your messing up the house, maybe you could give the lessons outside. If she's worried about your schoolwork, maybe you could get it done as soon as you get home from school. If nothing you say answers her concerns? Accept it. Blow off some steam with a run around the block, come back, sit down, and start working on a new idea.

Problems with partners

You and Allison were going to have so much fun. Instead you're at each other's throats. She says you're bossy, but SHE isn't doing enough work!

Have you two ever talked about who is responsible for what? If not, do. Write it all down in a partnership agreement. Sometimes just making everything clear is enough to ease the tension. Then again, if Allison just doesn't have the time or interest in the business that you have, it's best to recognize that. A person who does 25% of the work should get 25% of the profits—not half. If Allison won't agree to that, you might need to find a different partner. Just keep your cool as you talk things through. You don't want losing a partner to mean losing a friend.

Poor sales
You've sold just one hat in three hours. What's wrong?

Talk to people: they'll tell you. Maybe your hats cost more than your potential customers are willing to pay. Maybe they don't like the design. Maybe your stand is in the wrong place, so too few people see it. Once you know what the problem is, you can address it.

Unfair?
Everything was going great. You were selling 15 bracelets a week. Then Breeana up and starts to sell bracelets, too. Isn't there a law against this kind of thing?

Nope. It's called competition. Don't let it rattle you. Make it a challenge instead. Compare your bracelets and Breeana's. Does she have a better clasp? Improve your own. Are yours more stylish? Good! Make them even more so. Can you charge less than she does? Advertise? Put a cute tag on your bracelets so that everybody knows where they came from? How about branching out with matching necklaces? Think of all the ways you can make your crafts a better buy, and Breeana will be scrambling to keep up.

Too nice

You sell dog booties. They take two hours to make and the material costs you $4.50. You charge $12 for them at craft fairs. Now Penelope comes over and says, "Your booties are so cute! I really, really want some for my dog Argus. Could you sell me a set for four dollars? Pretty please?"

Don't do it. You are asking a reasonable amount for a product you worked hard on. Penelope has no business trying to cajole you into feeling sorry for her or guilty about making the profit you deserve. So say, "I'm sorry, but it wouldn't be fair to my other customers."

World domination

Never, ever did you imagine that so many parents would want to send their little kids to your story-telling hour. You had to start a second hour, and now you've got enough people on your waiting list to start a third. Three storytelling hours! There goes the rest of your life. Maybe you should just pull the plug on this whole idea.

You could. But you could also expand your business. Talk to a friend about running that third storytelling hour. Have her visit one of your sessions. Give her a chance to read a little, too. Once you're convinced she'll do a good job, call those people on your waiting list. Tell them you've taken on a partner, and you two are offering a free introductory story hour at your house. If that goes well, your friend can start holding that third hour at her own house.

let's go shopping!

the wonderful world of shopping

It's Saturday. You've got friends at your side, a purse with some cash, and the mall at your feet. You're happy—even a little excited—walking along under the bright lights, listening to music and the babble of voices. The air smells of pretzels and cookies and pizza. You love being here, talking to friends about what you like and don't like. You don't have to buy anything to have a good time. And yet—funny—you often do. How's that work?

In fact, when you're in a mall, you're in a landscape very different from the rest of the world. There are **no windows to the outdoors.** Blue sky, fresh air, dirt, pavement—that all sort of disappears. What you have instead are signs, lighting, colors, advertisements, and stylish displays.

It's a landscape designed by people who have one thing in mind: encouraging you to buy things. Everything is arranged to that purpose.

For example, almost every store has small, cheap items on the counter **by the cash register** tempting you to buy more as you stand in line waiting to check out.

In a grocery store, the things most people need, like milk, will be **toward the back.** That way, you have to walk past a bunch of other stuff to get there and are more likely to grab something else as well.

In a department store, the **first floor** is generally full of cosmetics, handbags, scarves, and jewelry—small things that storeowners want you to see when you come in to get new jeans.

Even how things are shelved can make a difference. The items **placed at eye level** are the items that the storeowners most want you to notice. The best deal might be on the bottom shelf, where you have to bend down to see it.

There are a **hundred other gimmicks** the stores use to encourage you to open that purse. The more aware you are of how such places work, the less likely you are to go home with a bag, look inside, and think, "Now, why'd I buy *that?*"

best buys, worst buys

Have you ever been really happy—or unhappy—with a purchase? You're not alone. Here's what some girls had to say about their best buys ever—and their worst.

What was your best buy ever?

"A hand-knit sweater. It was beautiful and made any outfit look great."
Leia

"Beads for my friends, because they like it when I make bracelets for them."
Liz

"A fund-raiser through my church to send money to kids who can't go to the doctor. The feeling of helping someone in need was great."
Antonia

"A notebook. As silly as that seems, it's a very good notebook. It's hard-covered and is lined on only one side, leaving the other side to illustrate."
Elizabeth

"A puppy, because I love her very much. She's always been there for me no matter what."
Emily

What was your worst buy?

"These shoes that were a little too small.
I still bought them because that was the
shoe everyone was wearing. They were so
expensive. They hurt my feet really bad.
That didn't matter then. Well, now it does."
Claire

"A portable DVD player. I bought it
with a bunch of money that I'd earned,
and then later I realized that there
was a cheaper version for half price. I
should have bought the less expensive
one. I rarely use the one I have now."
Morgan

"Candy. It's gone in a second."
Karyn

"When I was nine, I saved up all my birthday
money to buy what looked like a huge purple
couch. So I ordered it and when it came, I
had to crouch down to sit in it, and when it
folded out into a bed, my feet were sticking
out three feet off the end."
Melissa

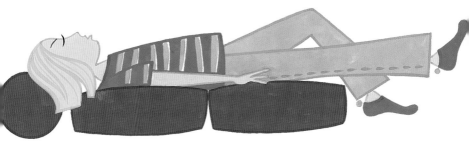

what kind of shopper are you?

What sounds most like you? Circle your answers.

1. What a deal! Two calendars featuring your favorite actor. Then you realize that they're for this year. Hmm. It's October. You:

   a. **get yourself both calendars. Hey, they'll work for two months.**

   b. **look through next year's calendars. Maybe you'll come back in February and some will be on sale.**

2. You have slippers already. True. But *yours* aren't shaped like Felix the Cat. And for $5.95? You:

   a. **grab a pair and head for the register.**

   b. **picture how warm your feet are in your other slippers and walk on by.**

3. You're at the checkout with a daisy-bead curtain for your room. Then you see it: a foot-long pen with an ostrich feather on the end. Oh. My. Golly. Would that pen look cool on your desk or what? You wrap your fist around it and:

   a. **pay for it.**

   b. **wave it in the air, tell yourself that the thing is too big to actually use (which it is), and put it back.**

4. Never, ever have you seen something as adorable as this stuffed dog. It looks like it's sleeping, and it breathes. And—get this—it comes in a *pet purse.* Too cute! You:

   a. **buy it right now with the money you were saving to upgrade your computer.**

   b. **decide to wait. By the time you're home, you're thinking about all you'll be able to do with a better computer.**

5. Your mom gave you $25 and told you to pick out some nice pants and a shirt for the trip to your grandparents'. While you're checking the racks, you come across a stack of spaghetti-string tops. You:

   a. **put one on the pile. You can wear it under the shirt at Grandma's.**

   b. **buy only the clothes you know you need.**

6. You pick out a nail-care set for your friend's birthday. It has everything she could want. Nearby is a display case full of single jars of glitter polish. You:

   a. **buy yourself a bottle. With your friend getting so much, shouldn't you be able to get something, too?**

   b. **check out the different colors of polish but buy only the gift.**

7. Garage sales are super! Where else would you find a gumball machine for $3? Sure, it's broken. But you could fix it. Maybe. You:

   a. **hand over the money, spend an hour trying to figure out why the thing won't work, and then throw it away.**

   b. **pick up an unused pumpkin candle for a quarter instead. You don't exactly need that, either, but it smells yummy.**

8. "A cherry soda, please," you say at the counter. But wait. Your friends are thirsty, too—thirsty and broke. You:

   a. **say, "Make it five."**

   b. **get some extra straws so your friends can each have a sip.**

54

Answers

Free spender

If you answered mostly **a's,** you spend money freely—maybe too freely. You satisfy your urge to buy even when it leads you to spend money on things you don't need. Is the item a lot like something you already have? Are you buying more than you really need? Does the thing have any real value? Are you keeping your long-term goals in mind? Those are the kinds of questions you need to ask yourself to put on the brakes.

Money minder

If you answered mostly **b's,** you know you can get what you want without spending money. You're glad to share, borrow, and adapt what you have—you withstand buying temptations. When the big stuff comes along that you *really* want, you'll be ready.

shop smart

A savvy shopper gets more for her money. Be one.

Needs and wants
You may *want* all kinds of things: new lip gloss, a chocolate milk shake, a charm bracelet, purple high-tops. But you don't *need* them in the way you might need, say, a white shirt for the chorus performance or food for your hamster or a birthday gift for your dad. Be aware of the difference between needs and wants. Before you spend money on the optional things, be sure you have the most important stuff covered.

Compare
Don't buy the first item you see. If you're in the market for some socks, look at several different brands and visit more than one store. How do the socks you see compare in style and quality? How about prices? Socks packaged at two for $5.99 are more expensive than socks packaged at four for $8.99, though if the socks in the four-pack seem thin and poorly made, they still may not be the better deal.

Ask questions
If you don't see what you want, ask about it: "Do you carry leotards?"

Go for the bargains
Go to the back of the store. That's where the discount racks will be. Ask about upcoming sales, too. You can save a lot by waiting for things to go on sale, especially when it comes to big purchases.

Give it a try

If you can, do. If you're buying shoes, try on more than one size and walk around the store. Take your time to be sure they really fit. If you're thinking about buying a CD that has a song you particularly like, see if you can sample it online or in a store. Better yet, borrow a friend's. After two days of listening, you may have heard enough.

Do your homework

If you've been saving for two years to get a computer, you want to be sure you get the best one your money can buy. A salesman can be helpful, but his job is to sell you things. Do your own research. Talk with people who have made a similar purchase. Learn from their mistakes. Check out publications that do product research, like *Consumer Reports*.

Avoid impulse buys

You may love that poncho at this moment. Fair enough. But you don't need it. So put it back on the rack and wait a few days. If that "I gotta have it" feeling passes, you'll be glad you held off.

Return it

Make it a habit: save receipts, and don't remove the tags on something you've bought for at least a day. Stores have different policies about returns (it's good to ask before you buy), and special rules apply to sales. But most of the time, the best fix for a bum purchase is to take it back.

six ways not to buy

Red light!

You've got a purple plastic monkey in your hand. It's useless, but, boy, is it cute! You want it. You're moving toward the cash register. You know you're going to regret this. Aaaah! How do you stop yourself?

Make way for the wise girl who lives in your head. She has a few questions for you.

1. Do you need this? Really? Why? What are you going to do with it?

2. Think of a person whose judgment you admire. Your mom or dad, your brother Ryan or your godmother Rae. What would they say about spending money on this monkey?

3. Picture yourself and this monkey a month from now. Are you going to think it's so all-fired cute then? Or will it be in a bin in the basement?

4. Think of some bad buys you've made. Line those items up in your brain along with the monkey. Seem similar? That's a bad sign.

5. Imagine life without this monkey. Would it be any worse than life with it? Then why buy the thing?

6. You were saving up money so you could get a new bike, correct? Then picture that bike. Hold it in your mind as you set down that monkey and walk out of the store. Chances are good that you'll feel happier with yourself with every step.

spending spree

You got $75 for your birthday from your Uncle Jerome. "I want you to spend this," he said. So off you go to the mall with your pals. What do you do when you get there? Keep track of what you have left as you go.

1. You've been at the mall for an hour. "I'm starved," says your friend. "I'm going to Palacio del Taco." You tag along and:

   a. **get a taco, too.** $.89

   b. **get the Supremo Special, with three crispy tacos (and eat one and a half).** $4.69

   c. **sit with your friend but eat nothing. You ate before you came.** $0

$75.00

minus _____
(answer #1)

equals _____
(money remaining)

2. You love this singer. There on the display is her newest CD. You:

   a. **snap it up.** $12.99

   b. **borrow the CD from a friend.** $0

   c. **go to a different store where music is cheaper and you can sample songs from CDs you're interested in. There are a bunch of songs you like, so you buy the CD.** $10.99

_____
(money remaining from above)

minus _____
(answer #2)

equals _____
(money remaining)

3. Last year's sandals just don't look very exciting. You:

  a. get some plastic daisies to snazz them up. $6.95

  b. buy new sandals. $12.99

  c. buy two pairs. With so many colors, it was too hard to make up your mind. $24.98

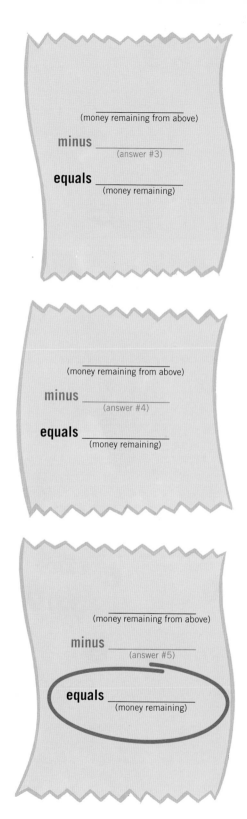

_____
(money remaining from above)

minus _____
(answer #3)

equals _____
(money remaining)

4. You're totally out of nail polish—and you're a girl who likes nail polish. You get:

  a. Four bottles. $11.82

  b. One. $4.98

  c. Three. $7.79

_____
(money remaining from above)

minus _____
(answer #4)

equals _____
(money remaining)

5. On the way home, you stop to get you and your friends some treats. When you've unloaded your goods at the register, the clerk rings up:

  a. microwave popcorn and a liter of soda. $3.58

  b. microwave popcorn, some brownie mix, and a 12-pack of soda. $10.22

  c. microwave popcorn, some brownie mix, a 24-pack of soda, a cake, a box of ice cream bars, a package of curly straws, a 12-pack of gum, and two cat toys. $20.52

_____
(money remaining from above)

minus _____
(answer #5)

equals _____
(money remaining)

How much money do you have left?

$0
You had a big day. Once you've finished your snacks, you'll have a CD, two pairs of new sandals, four bottles of nail polish, and some straws and cat toys to show for it. Fair enough. Uncle Jerome said spend, and you did. But now you can hang up your purse. Big spending sprees can be fun, but they end early.

$1–$30
You bought a fair amount of stuff, but you also made some decisions that saved you money. You can go back to the store you passed on the way in and get the cute stockings you admired earlier. You might even have enough for a book.

$30 or more
You're a girl who gets the most bang possible from a buck. If you don't need to spend to get what you want, you don't do it. When you do spend, you want value (maybe you even noticed three for $7.79 was the best deal on nail polish). After a day at the mall, you're still in a position to buy something big. When you write your thank-you note to Uncle Jerome, you can say you had your shopping spree and still have money to put away for the next one.

how gullible are you?

There are lots of ways people are persuaded to spend money they never intended to spend. Could this be you? Yes or no?

1. When you want clothes, this is the place you go. It's expensive, and the clerks aren't very nice. But the people in the banner out front look so cool and so happy. You just love going in here.

Yes   No

2. You're in the bowling alley, putting quarters into a glass box with a little claw hovering over a bin of toys. You've tried the game three times already. If you can make the claw go just the tiniest bit slower, the pink walrus will be yours! You go get more change.

Yes   No

3. The waiter smiles. "You want dessert with that? We have the best banana cream pie." Pie! Now that you think of it, pie sure sounds good.

Yes   No

4. This CD isn't sold in stores. You have to call a 1-800 number on TV. It must be really special! You'd be the only kid to have it.

Yes   No

5. Not only does this bath gel make your skin softer, it will make your brain cells more elastical. It says so on the label. You'll be more intelligent and do better at school.

Yes   No

Answers

If you answered **yes,** here's what you need to know:

1. Advertising is all about creating a world that the customer admires. Often, that means photographs populated by beautiful people, celebrities, and sports stars, all of whom seem to be having a lot of fun or falling in love (or both). You may have seen ads for this store of yours on TV, in magazines, on billboards. It's pretty impossible not to be affected by all that. But you can be aware of it. Resist!

You can go ahead and go to this store. But make yourself look at the same kind of item at a less expensive store as well. Compare the two. Block out everything else. If you would be fine with the cheaper shirt if it were on the rack at the glamorous store, that's the one you should buy.

2. You're buying the right to take a chance. What kind of chance is it? Lousy. If you don't believe it, stand back and watch other people plugging quarters into the machine. You'll find they spend twice as much trying to get that walrus than they would if they walked across the street and bought the stuffed platypus on display at the drugstore.

3. Businesses make a lot of money by planting ideas in people's heads. "Do you want fries with that?" "Would you like to see these earrings?" "Black stockings would go well with that skirt. Shall I show you some?" Don't let someone else do your thinking for you.

4. There's something about 1-800 numbers that appeals to people. Would this CD stand out to you if it were on a shelf with hundreds of others at the local discount store? Not likely.

5. Beware of a product that promises to deliver more than your own common sense tells you it can. Pigs don't fly, and bath gel won't improve your grades. It might make you smell nice, but it's just bath gel.

plastic money

As you've surely noticed, people often don't buy things with cash. They buy them with plastic cards. There are two basic kinds of cards:

A **debit card** simply gets money from your bank account to the store where you are making a purchase. It lets you spend your money without having to carry it with you. (More about this in the next chapter.)

A **credit card** lets you borrow money, usually from a bank. That is, the store gets the money you owe not from your account but from the bank itself. At the end of the month, that bank adds up all the purchases you made on your credit card and sends you a bill. You can pay that bill right then, or you can pay just a little bit of what you owe and pay the rest later.

Sweet deal! Right?

Not necessarily.

Credit cards and debit cards both make life easier, but there is a BIG difference. Interest.

Credit-card companies don't lend you money to be nice. They do it to make money. They make that money by charging you a little extra for every dollar you borrow that you don't repay right away. That extra is called **interest.**

On small amounts, interest may seem like no big deal. But it can be an extremely big deal if you continue to put new charges on a credit card and avoid paying the entire amount, which is what many people do. Credit cards make it so easy to keep spending long after you should stop.

What happens to a person who racks up $1,000 in charges on her credit card and then pays it off $25 at a time? She could end up paying $500 in interest, that's what. In fact, there are instances where people actually spend *more* in interest than they spent on the stuff to begin with.

It's a big old trap that the credit-card companies would be only too happy for you to fall into. So don't. If you buy a $25 bracelet, pay $25. Don't avoid paying for it for so long that the same bracelet ends up costing you $35 instead.

Don't spend more money than you have. It's that simple.

saving
money

get in the habit

You want a new printer in the worst way. It costs $120 and you have $0. How do you get from $0 to $120? Smart shopping alone won't do it. Saving can.

Saving is a habit, and like any other habit, it takes a while to establish. Here are some saving tips from girls like you:

"Take two coffee cans. Cut a slot in the top of each of them. Label one SPEND and the other SAVE. When you get allowance or any money, put half of it in SPEND and the other half in SAVE. Put more in SAVE if you are saving up for something special. You can only empty SAVE once a month. (If you are saving up for something, make it longer!)"
Cara

"I started saving money by putting my money in the bank. Then it's hard to get it out without Mom and Dad."
Allie

"A good way to save money is by keeping the change. Say you bought an ice cream and got $2.78 back. Put the 78 cents into a savings jar. You can save a lot of money by keeping your change."
Megan

"Don't take money with you when you're shopping. If you don't have it, you can't spend it!"
Karen

"If you keep your money in a piggy bank or wallet, tape a picture of something big you really want on top. Every time you reach for money, you will see the picture and remember to save your money."
Jenny

Of course, it also helps to have a real plan for how to reach your goal. So think the thing through:

My saving goal

Computer printer: $120

If I could save $10 a month
$120 \div 10 = 12$ months
I could buy my printer in a year.

If I could save $20 a month
$120 \div 20 = 6$ months
I could buy my printer
by the time school starts.

Six months: not bad! *Could* you save that much regularly? To answer that one, you first need to know how much you're making and spending now. You need a budget.

budgeting basics

A **budget** is a plan for how to use your money.

To make a budget that works for you, start by writing down how much money you earn or receive on average every month. You might earn nothing one month and a lot the next, so you'll need to keep track for a while to get a good answer. Be sure to include your allowance and gift money, too.

At the same time, start keeping track of how much money you spend on food, entertainment, and everything else. Save receipts (toss them into a shoe box) and write everything down.

Subtract what you spend from what you earn to find how much you save now in an average month.

How's that number look? Do you want to save more? Then maybe you can spend less on CDs and movies. Maybe you can earn more, too. Make some decisions, put it all together, and you've got your budget:

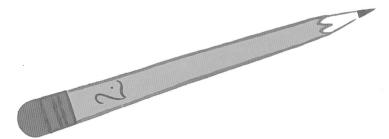

Budget

What I expect to earn or receive every month

My allowance **$25**
(counting the raise I got from doing new chores)

Profits from my moneymaker **$30**
(if I sell two more scarves a week)

Gift money **$5**

Total **$60**
($10 more than I get now)

What I plan to spend every month

Food, movies, and entertainment **$15**

CDs and clothes **$12**

Charity, gifts, and other things **$8**

Total **$35**
($10 less than I spend now)

What I plan to save

Total monthly savings: **$25**
I'll put **$20** toward my printer and
$5 in long-term savings.

See? It's all there in your budget plan! Now all you need to do is stick to it.

beyond piggy banks

Now that you're saving seriously, you may want to put your piggy bank out to pasture and open a simple savings account at a bank or credit union.

How's it work? You give the bank your money and they give you a **register,** a little booklet that helps you keep track of your money now that you can't dump it on the bed to count it.

From now on, if you want to put more money in the account, you can go to the bank and fill out a deposit slip.

SAVINGS DEPOSIT

NAME *Catherine Medici*

ACCT.NO. *000001*

DATE *7/28/06*

Catherine M edici

SIGN HERE FOR CASH RECEIVED (IF REQUIRED)

Lottamoney National Bank

1 2 3 4 5 6 7 8 9

CASH	CURRENCY	2 0	00
	COIN		50
CHECKS		1 0	00
	TOTAL FROM OTHER SIDE		
	TOTAL	3 0	50
	LESS CASH RECEIVED	5	00
	NET DEPOSIT	2 5	50

If you receive a check from someone, **endorse** it by signing your name on the back, then record the amount on the slip. If you want some money back in cash, record that, too. On all bank forms, fill in the entire amount, including the cents, even if they are zeros.

When you want to get some of your money out of your account, you fill out a similar slip for withdrawals.

In either case, write down what you're doing in your register. Always subtract or add to find out what you have in your account right now. That's called your **balance.**

DATE	EXPLANATION	(-) WITHDRAWAL	(+) DEPOSIT	(+) INTEREST	BALANCE
					75.74
3/1	babysitting money		25.50		101.24
3/10	spending money for trip	15.00			86.24
3/25	birthday gift		30.00		116.24
3/29	video game	40.00			76.24

cash cards

Of course, people don't always go to the bank to move their money around. More and more adults do a lot of their banking online. And by far the most common way to get money out of an account is with an ATM card.

Ah, ATMs! You've surely seen your parents punch a few magic numbers into the neighborhood Automated Teller Machine and drive off with a stack of bills. Once you have a bank account of your own, you might get an ATM card, too.

Every ATM card has a secret number called a PIN, or Personal Identification Number. To use the card, you have to type in your PIN. Your PIN protects you from theft. If somebody else tried to use your card, he couldn't do it if he didn't know your number. So be sure to keep your PIN a secret.

If your ATM card is also a debit card, you can use it to buy things. (Remember, unlike a credit card, a debit card sends money to the store directly from your bank account, much as if you were writing a check.)

Such convenience!

Such possibilities!

Just one problem: you don't want to get carried away and spend more than you actually have in your account. When that happens, you're overdrawn. The bank will charge you a fee—a big one.

The solution? Carry your account register with you wherever you carry the debit card. Pull the register out while you're paying at the counter and write down your purchase right then, right there. Not in the food court. Not in the car on the way home. Not in your room that night. Write it down before you take a step out of the store.

making money with money

So, what's the bank doing with your money when you're not around? It's using it. Banks make money with money. They loan money to people and charge them interest. Banks also invest money in all kinds of ways.

And get this: You can do the same thing. Once you've saved money, you can put it to work making more money. Here are just a few of the options:

Interest accounts
Banks pay you for the privilege of using your money. Interest rates vary from year to year and account to account. On a simple savings account, you won't get much. But something's better than nothing.

Certificates of deposit (CDs)
A CD is similar to a savings account, only you can't take your money out for a certain, agreed-upon period of time, so you get more interest. And more interest = more money.

Savings bonds
When you were born, someone might have bought a savings bond for you, knowing that by the time you were headed for college, that bond could be worth more than twice the amount paid. A person who buys a savings bond is lending money to the government.

Stocks

When you buy stock, you're buying a little bit of a business. The value of your stock may go up and down from one day to the next, a bit like a roller coaster, but over time, if the business grows and makes money, you can make money, too—a lot more than you would get if you left your money in a simple savings account.

Then again, if the business does poorly, you can lose money. It's even possible to lose all your money. Some stocks are a lot safer than others, but no stock is 100% guaranteed.

Mutual funds

A mutual fund is like a basket full of different stocks. Buy a share of a mutual fund and you are buying a little bit of a lot of different companies.

how to become
a millionaire

You've worked and saved, and you've got yourself $1,000. What can you do with it? Just look!

If you can get a 5% return on that money through your investments, in 10 years that $1,000 becomes $1,629. And if you keep on saving, in 50 years that $1,000 becomes $11,467.

Get the picture? It's like a snowball going downhill. The longer you let it ride, the bigger it gets. A person who starts saving when she's young has a big, big advantage. Simply by choosing to invest that $1,000 rather than spend it, you could have more than $10,000.

Better yet: say you get a job when you're a teenager and you start saving $1,000 every year.

If you can get a 5% return on that money through investments, in 10 years it'll be worth $12,578. And if you keep it up for 50 years, it's at $209,348.

AND . . .

(sound the trumpets)

if you can manage to save $1,000 a year and get a return of 10%—the historical average for the stock market—

in 50 years you will have more than $1,160,000. That's right. More than **one million** dollars. If you start saving now, you could be a millionaire.

twenty dollars

So what does it mean, "rich"?

Say you earned $20 selling paper fans at a swim meet. What's that $20 mean to you? Chances are, it seems more valuable than the money your grandmother sent for your birthday because you worked so hard to earn it. But suppose you'd expected to earn $30 off those paper fans. Then you might feel disappointed. And if you expected to earn only $10? Then you might feel rich.

It's not really about the $20, is it?

It's about expectations.

Most of us look at the money we have in terms of

the money we expected to have,

the money other people have,

the money we're used to having.

It's also about attitude.

Is $20 a lot or a little? Is the glass half-empty or half-full? It depends on how you look at it.

Keep this in mind now that you're going to start earning and saving money of your own. Aim as high as high can be for your future, but don't expect to get there overnight. Make the goals you're working on right now realistic. And keep your mind focused on the money you have, not on the money you don't.

"Rich" is often in the eye of the beholder. There will always be people who have more than you, just as there will always be people who have less. The difference is what you do with what you have.

81

two dollars

Two bucks. If you were going to spend it, what could you get? Two liters of soda? A jumbo candy bar? A string bracelet? Not a whole lot.

Yet in fact, nearly half the people on the planet live on less than two dollars a day. That's all they have to spend on everything they need—shelter, heat, food, shoes and shirts, doctors and medicine, transportation. You name it.

Which brings us to giving and charity.

Some people find that one of the greatest pleasures of having money is being able to give some of it away. For them, giving is as much a part of managing money as earning, spending, and saving.

Just what can money do? For starters:

For $12 you could feed 17 people a meal at a local food pantry.

For $20 you could buy a flock of baby chicks for a family in Africa, which would provide those people with 200 eggs a year (not to mention meat, fertilizer for the garden, and more chickens).

For $18 a month you and your Scout troop could help support a specific child in Asia or South America—a child with whom you could exchange greetings and photographs.

There are organizations that provide care for the elderly, feed and educate children, build homes for the homeless, fund schools and hospitals, and supply disaster relief to people when terrible things happen.

Do you like animals? You might look into groups devoted to saving endangered species or helping abandoned pets.

Are you concerned about the environment? You could support efforts to clean up our water or our air, to preserve the wilderness here in America, or to protect rain forests on the other side of the globe.

The list of good causes is endless. Get involved in charitable giving, and it's hard to go wrong. Doing good feels good. And you'll be helping to create a better, healthier, more peaceful world for everyone, including you. What better way to use money could there be?

one girl

Here you are, heading off toward tomorrow and the day after that. No matter where you stand, the road to financial security starts directly under your feet. You know the signs that mark the rest of the way:

Pay attention to your money.

Be willing to work (and have fun doing it).

Save first.

Make a budget.

Know the difference between needs and wants.

Don't spend more than you have.

Grow good habits.

Invest.

That's it. That's the path you want to follow. Stick to it and what you'll have in the end is **freedom**—freedom to do as you like, go where you choose, and live as you most want to live. Of all the big, fat, fabulous opportunities out there waiting for you beyond the horizon, there are few as wonderful as that.

85

101 money-making ideas*

*Every good business needs a good plan. Be sure to talk to your parents before you start.

do chores and odd jobs

1 When the neighbors are out of town, water their plants,

2 feed their pets, 3 take in the mail,

4 or water their grass.

5 Plant gardens 6 or weed them.

7 Mow lawns

8 or rake leaves.

9 Shovel snow.

TIP: Ask if you can put a sign in a snowbank by the curb advertising your business.

10 Help a neighbor spread mulch.

11 Be a golf caddy.

12 Do pool maintenance.

13 Run errands for an elderly couple or a busy parent with a long commute.

14 Wrap gifts at Christmastime.

15 Pack boxes for people who are moving.

16 Clip coupons from the newspaper and organize them for your mom or the neighbor next door.

17 Paint mailboxes **18** or fences.

19 Paint house numbers on curbs.

20 Set out garbage or
21 organize someone's recycling.

22 Run somebody's garage sale (maybe your own).

take on the dirty work

23 Clean pet cages **24** or aquariums.

25 Muck stalls.

26 Clean basements
27 or kitchens.

28 Clean cars
29 or boats
30 or patios.

31 Wash windows (not high ones).

32 Pick up backyard dog doo.

33 Organize the neighbors' garage
34 or their closets.

35 Serve food at parties
36 or arrive afterward and clean up.

use your skills

37 **Tutor** younger kids in your favorite subject.

38 **Teach** an elderly person to use a computer.

39 **Make** Web pages for your little sister's Brownie troop.

40 **Design** a newsletter for the rec program

41 or a brochure for your brother's bike-repair business.

42 **Teach** piano, **43** tennis,
44 sewing, **45** or tap dancing.

46 **Ref** soccer games.

47 **Be** a director. Find some fun scripts
(or write one yourself) and put on a play
with the neighborhood kids.

48 **Be** a personal trainer. Run a mile a
day with the little boy next door so that
he's ready for hockey season.

49 **Paint** faces with face paint at the street fair.

50 **Paint** other girls' nails.

51 **Take** "best friend" pictures for kids at school.

52 **Make movies** of school plays
53 or talent shows,
54 of your brother's middle-school
graduation
55 or other family events.

> **TIP: Movie-making can be a terrific business. A coach might want a movie of her team's season to show at the final banquet. The head of the day camp might want a movie to show parents what kinds of activities are offered there. A young couple might want a movie of their new baby to send to Grandma in Cleveland.**

56 **Make** scrapbooks for people who don't have
time to do it themselves.

57 **Do** bike tune-ups.

58 **Tie** balloon hats and animals at birthday parties.

care for others

59 Babysit.

60 Be a counselor at a day camp

61 or a mother's helper.

> TIP: Parents with a new baby might be eager to have you around to play with the baby's toddler brother, so he'll be happy and out of mischief.

62 Keep an elderly neighbor company.

63 Be a kid wrangler, and help out at a toddler's birthday party.

64 Or organize children's parties yourself, from invites to thank-yous.

65 Run a story hour at your house. Tell parents they can drop off their kids and you'll read them stories and serve snacks.

66 Do the same things with crafts **67** or games.

68 Provide after-school entertainment for somebody's cats.

69 Walk dogs

70 or groom them.

make things and sell them

71 Hot drinks at the soccer game.

72 Cold drinks at the swim meet.

73 Paper-clip jewelry.

74 Bird feeders.

75 Yard signs ("Thanks for slowing down" is always popular.)

76 Banners to welcome people home or celebrate birthdays.

77 Hand-designed T-shirts,

78 key chains,

79 or zipper pulls.

80 Pet treats,

81 cat toys,

82 or personalized pet food dishes.

83 High-energy snacks made of nuts and chocolate morsels.

84 Sponge-print wrapping paper.

85 Sleeping bags for the little stuffed toys that all your friends are collecting this year.

TIP: What's the biggest fad at your school? Think of things you can make that relate to it.

86 Flowers cut from a garden you plant and tend yourself.

87 Badges that promote school spirit.

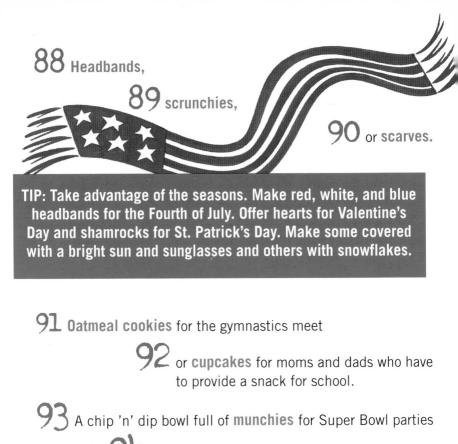

88 Headbands,

89 scrunchies,

90 or **scarves.**

TIP: Take advantage of the seasons. Make red, white, and blue headbands for the Fourth of July. Offer hearts for Valentine's Day and shamrocks for St. Patrick's Day. Make some covered with a bright sun and sunglasses and others with snowflakes.

91 **Oatmeal cookies** for the gymnastics meet

92 or **cupcakes** for moms and dads who have to provide a snack for school.

93 A chip 'n' dip bowl full of **munchies** for Super Bowl parties

94 or **gingerbread houses** at Christmas.

TIP: Be creative. Make a traditional gingerbread house but offer a gingerbread doghouse with a satellite dish, too. Buyers who resist the first might go for the second.

95 **Christmas wreaths,**

96 **ornaments,**

97 or **cookies.**

98 **Decorated tins** full of chocolate kisses with cards to match celebrating Valentine's Day,

99 Mother's Day,

100 Father's Day,

101 or birthdays.

Have you discovered a new way to make money? Got a great tip for other girls on saving—or spending—money? Share it!

Write to:
American Girl
Money Editor
8400 Fairway Place
Middleton, WI 53562

All comments and ideas submitted may be used by American Girl without compensation or acknowledgment.

Here are some other American Girl books you might like:

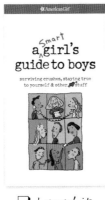

❏ I read it.

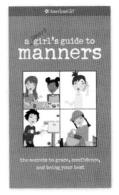

❏ I read it.

❏ I read it.

❏ I read it.

❏ I read it.